AIR DEFENSE WEAPONS

AIR DEFENSE WEAPONS

by John Nicholas

Rourke Enterprises, Inc.
Vero Beach, Florida 32964

Air defense is frequently a one-on-one engagement — one man
against one aircraft — with only seconds to aim and fire.

Library of Congress Cataloging-in-Publication Data

Nicholas, John, 1944-
    Air defense weapons/by John Nicholas.   p. cm. —
    (The Army library)
    Includes index.
    Summary: Describes the different kinds of air defense weapons used by the United States Army at various times in history, including radar, anti-aircraft guns, and missiles.
    ISBN 0-86592-423-6
    1. United States — Air defenses, Military — Juvenile literature. 2. United States. Army — Weapons systems — Juvenile literature. [1. United States — Air defenses, Military. 2. United States. Army-Weapons systems.]
I. Title. II. Series: Nicholas, John, 1944- Army library.
UG733.N53   1989   623.3-dc19   88-32665
                                           CIP
                                          AC

CONTENTS

AIR DEFENDERS

The highly agile A-10 Thunderbolt, seen here during a training mission, poses a major threat to enemy ground targets.

Today we think of military aircraft carrying out long-range bombing missions, fighting duels in the sky high above the ground, or attacking shore targets from aircraft carriers. Planes do all of these things and more. Yet the duty of military aircraft when they were first used long ago was to spy for the troops on the ground and to provide information about what the enemy was doing.

The role of **airborne reconnaissance** was by far the most important during World War One (1914-18). The more exciting fighter planes fought each other or looked for reconnaissance planes to shoot down. Although their job was not as glamorous as the fighter pilots' job, the airmen who manned the reconnaissance planes were much more useful to the forces on the ground.

In World War One, the aircraft was seen as a threat because of the information its pilot would gather. Efforts were made to shoot down these spies in the sky. Some attempts were successful, and Germany's leading fighter ace, Baron Manfred von Richthofen, is thought by some to have been shot down and killed by a machine gun on the ground.

In World War Two (1939-45), the aircraft developed into a remarkable fighting machine. The fortunes of the armies on the ground depended very often on who had control of the air. Planes designed to attack tanks, artillery, and troops could be more than just a nuisance. They could destroy important targets and hold back armed units assembling for an advance. Because of this, anti-aircraft guns were quickly developed and put into operation.

This AH-64 Apache attack helicopter is firing 2.75-inch rockets during tests.

When the United States and its allies liberated western Europe at the end of World War Two, the German air force lost control of the air. From that moment on, the German army was continually attacked from the air and was never again able to organize a major response with its armored units. The allies were able to gain ground quickly and take advantage of the confusion caused in the enemy ranks.

The Russians learned quickly the lessons of air attacks on ground forces. When Adolf Hitler, the Nazi German leader between 1933 and 1945, attacked Russia in 1941, he used air power to smash the Russian army. The Russians never forgot, and after the war they put a lot of effort into air-defense weapons. They have created what is today the world's biggest air-defense screen, using guns, rockets, and missiles to cover almost all of their national borders.

The United States learned the same lesson in the **Korean War** (1950-53), where U.S. aircraft came under very heavy fire from communist North Korean ground forces. In fact, of the approximately 1,000 U.S. planes shot down by the communists, almost 700 were lost to ground fire from army units that included both North Korean and Chinese forces. Only 110 or so were shot down by fighter planes.

The AH-64 attack helicopter can carry up to sixteen laser-guided anti-armor Hellfire missiles.

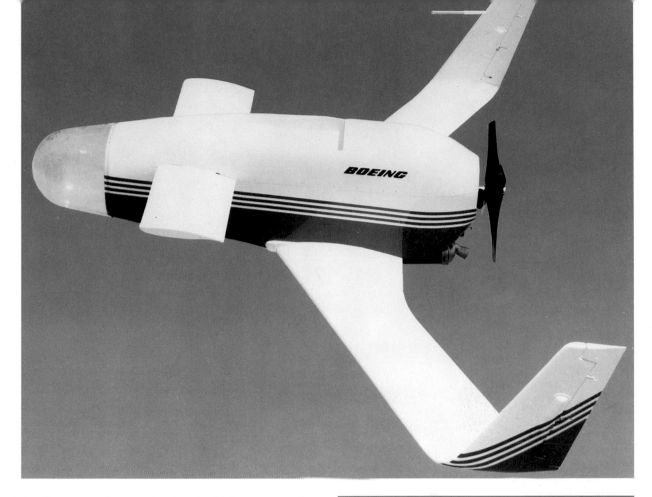

▲ Small, unmanned, remotely-piloted vehicles pose a serious threat to ground forces and must be quickly brought down before they can send back information on troop positions.

In the 1960s, when planes flew very high to escape gunfire from the ground, large missiles were developed to chase and destroy them. ▶

10

◄ The Nike family of surface-to-air missiles was first developed in the 1950s, when large numbers of Soviet aircraft were believed to pose a threat to Western defense.

The same pattern has emerged again and again since Korea. In the 1973 Middle East war between Israel and the Arab states, of 120 planes lost by the Israeli air force, almost 100 were shot down by ground defenses. Again, the Falklands war in 1982 showed exactly the same result. Of nine Harrier vertical-takeoff fighters lost by the British, five were shot down by Argentinian ground forces. The rest were lost in accidents, but not one was shot down by fighters.

Defending against air attack is very difficult, and the problems faced by air defense forces are enormous. Aircraft and helicopters attack at different heights, at different speeds, and under different conditions. Some will come in straight and low, gambling on sheer speed for escape. Others will keep close to the ground and maintain a relatively low speed using hills and folds in the surface of the earth to hide their approach.

Some helicopters hover in forest clearings, just the top of their weapons sensors peering above the trees, waiting like predators to strike armored columns or individual tanks. Other helicopters seek targets for the artillery, providing ground forces with information about range and accuracy.

Then there are **remotely piloted vehicles (RPVs)**, unmanned pilotless flying vehicles, about the size of large model planes. These pilotless flying machines are difficult to see and pose a real threat. They can spot the guns by sending TV pictures to fire control units on the ground, or they can provide pictures of targets for anti-tank planes to strike. The overwhelming abundance of airborne threats are all taken very seriously by the army.

Gunners with a Canadian anti-aircraft battery prepare to fire a Blowpipe surface-to-air guided missile on the edge of a military base during exercises in 1987.

TANK BUSTERS

The biggest threat to ground forces is the fast, low-flying **strike plane** that attacks ground targets with very little warning. These planes carry bombs and rockets and are very effective against tanks and fixed artillery sites. A typical ground attack plane is the Soviet MiG-27 Flogger D or J version. Capable of carrying more than 3 tons of weapons, the Flogger has a top speed of around 750 MPH at sea level. Flogger has a range of about 370 miles with external fuel tanks and a full weapons load.

Another type of high-speed air defense threat is the Soviet Sukhoi Su-24 Fencer with a top speed of 900 MPH at sea level. It too, can carry more than 3 tons of bombs and rockets, and with external fuel tanks it has a range of more than 800 miles. The Soviet air force operates about 1,400 MiG-27D/J and Su-24 ground attack planes in addition to 1,000 older types doing the same job less efficiently.

Similar aircraft operated by the U.S. Air Force are the F-111 fighter bomber and the F-4 Phantom. The most recent addition to the U.S. range of ground attack planes is the McDonnell Douglas F-15E Eagle, which has an astonishing carrying capacity of 11.5 tons of bombs and rockets over a strike range of 570 miles. One of the most effective ground attack planes in service in Europe is the Panavia Tornado, which can lift almost 10 tons of under-wing weapons a distance of 860 miles to the target.

It is important to make air defense systems as mobile as possible, since they must frequently be carried with the troops as they move from place to place.

◀ *Air defense equipment must be rugged enough to withstand rough handling as it is brought from ship to shore.*

Attack versions of this F-111, seen here during a training mission near Las Vegas, are some of the air force's major strike planes.
▼

During the mid-1980s, the air force took delivery of ground attack versions of the F-15 all-weather fighter.

Representing the other end of the speed range is the new generation of anti-armor planes specifically designed to hit tanks and armored vehicles hard and effectively. The United States was first in the field with the Republic A-10 Thunderbolt. This plane can loiter in the sky at very low speed and spends most of its life below 100 feet. It has a massive **gatling gun**, which is a collection of seven barrels strapped together firing at up to 4,200 rounds per minute. This gun is extremely effective against all types of tanks and armored vehicles.

The Soviet equivalent to the Eagle is the Sukhoi Su-25 Frogfoot. This plane appeared in the early 1980s and has been used in Afghanistan against rebel tribesmen opposed to the government. Frogfoot can carry 2 tons of bombs or rockets and has a range of approximately 180 miles. The appearance of this aircraft, specifically designed for low-speed ground attack, is sure proof that the Soviets recognize an aircraft's value in stopping enemy action on the ground.

Taken together, the fast, low-altitude strike planes and the slow, ground-hugging tank busters present a difficult target. Most weapons designed for defense against another weapon have a specific performance range. From a comparatively fixed point on the ground, however, units must be prepared to defend against incoming planes with wide performance capabilities. No single weapon exists that can defend ground units against all comers.

The most commonly used ground-attack weapons carried by high-speed strike planes are cluster bombs, armor-piercing high explosive bombs, or **napalm**. Cluster bombs are carried in canisters and released upon the target, usually to distribute lots of small explosives designed to penetrate concrete or destroy tanks, armored vehicles, fixed-wing planes, or helicopters. The canisters carry several hundred small bombs that eject their charges in a cluster.

Although air defense weapons for attacking fast-moving targets are usually purpose-built, the standard machine gun can be very useful when more sophisticated weapons are not to hand.

Aircraft coming in at 600 MPH, perhaps only 80 feet above the ground, would release cluster bombs less than a mile from the target. Ground defenders see the approaching aircraft as a tiny dot. Head on, the plane presents a very small target, and the gunners or missile operators have literally a few seconds to decide whether what they see is an enemy plane and whether they should attack it. It might provide a sense of satisfaction to hit the plane as it roars overhead or flies away, but by then it has done its job. The only sensible plan is to knock it out of action before it releases its weapons.

At the other end of the speed scale, helicopters pose a particularly serious problem because they are able to hide more easily and to release their weapons from concealed positions. Yet they carry all the punch and most of the fire power given out by the high-speed strike planes. They do not have the range, however, and cannot penetrate enemy defenses as readily as the high-speed attack plane does. For the tank crews, that knowledge is no compensation for a live missile coming straight at them.

Just a small group from the formidable range of weapons carried by a modern attack helicopter such as the AH-64 Apache.

Today's fast, modern attack helicopter poses a serious threat to tanks, armored vehicles, and infantry units. ▲

Large-scale movements of men and vehicles are also at risk when enemy air attacks threaten to destroy trains, bridges, and railheads.

SKY WATCHING

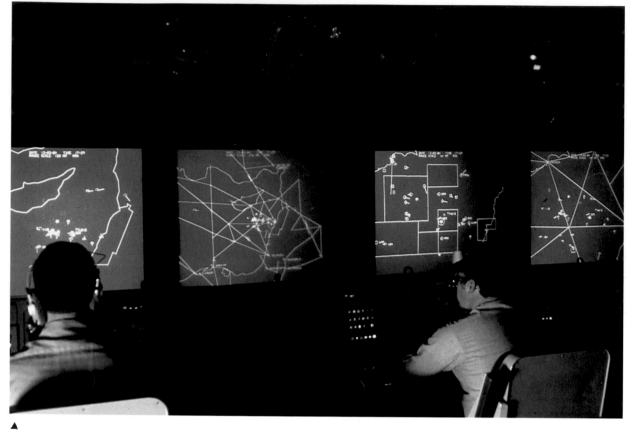

▲
Huge radar scanners keep watch over North American airspace, looking for signs of enemy attack or intruding aircraft; the information is displayed on large screens.

At the other end of the scale, small ground units need light, highly mobile radar "eyes" to locate and identify potential targets in the air. ▶

Air defense can be divided into three important stages, each of which leads to the next and all of which are vital and require separate items of equipment. First, the enemy must be seen and detected. Detection is not always easy and requires sophisticated electronic equipment used intelligently and with experience. Second, the object must be identified and categorized so that an appropriate weapon system, whether a gun or missile, can be chosen. Third, the weapon must be fired and the target destroyed.

Not every missile fired at an aircraft gets through and knocks the plane down. Achieving the third objective is much more difficult than it sounds, but no air defense system can get to that stage of the attack without completing the first two stages. Detection is a vital first link in the air defense chain and is usually accomplished with special **radar** sets on the ground looking for incoming enemy planes.

Radar is more effective than the human eye because it can detect aircraft a long distance away, and it does so more accurately. For instance, radar can detect an aircraft traveling at a height of 500 feet more than 25 miles away. The human eye could never pick up a relatively small strike plane at that distance, especially coming head on!

Air defense troops receive radar information to help them protect other ground forces, but they rely on computers to control the guns and missiles, which must be correctly programmed.

Air defense systems are not always light and easily transported; a large amount of equipment is needed to set up this Patriot air defense system.

◄ *Fast strike planes like these F-4 Phantoms would fly in at a very low altitude to give radar operators as little time as possible to locate, identify, and fire at them.*

Radar works by receiving reflected signals sent from an antenna. Using special frequencies within the wide range of radio frequencies, the antenna sends out a signal, sometimes in a particular direction and sometimes over a wide arc. Solid objects, such as aircraft, reflect radio waves. When these bounce back to the antenna, special electronic equipment can interpret that reflection as an incoming aircraft.

Radar detectors use frequencies that travel in straight lines. Because of that, the radar antenna must be as high as possible above ground to see long distances without obstruction. Because the antenna broadcasts a signal, the incoming plane is able to pick up that signal and tell the pilot or the navigator. The crew then knows they have been seen on an enemy radar screen and can expect imminent attack.

Most planes carry jamming devices that confuse the reflected signal, so that when it arrives back at the ground antenna the nature of the incoming target is not at all clear. Some planes expect radar to be switched on and send out jamming signals before they come within range of enemy antennas on the ground. Jammers can be quite sophisticated, changing the way the reflected signal is returned to the ground antenna. The antenna then

Despite its size, the Patriot air defense system is a great improvement on earlier systems, which required an even larger number of vehicles and much more ground support equipment. ▲

Remaining hidden and undetected is an important part of survival and radar equipment is protected by trees, bushes, and deceptive camouflage nets. ▼

"thinks" the incoming attacker is a flock of birds or a completely different type of aircraft altogether.

Ground radar detectors have an answer of their own, frequency-hopping. By switching the radar every few seconds through a range of different frequencies, "hopping" from one frequency to the other, the jammers on the attacker are avoided and the radar "sees" the plane as it really is. There is, however, also a way of getting around that. Some planes carry jammers that sweep through all known frequencies used by ground antennas, thoroughly confusing the picture altogether.

Achieving confusion in the mind of the enemy is better than trying to outrun anti-aircraft missiles. Throwing the enemy into a state of uncertainty is often enough to cause a brief lapse in judgement, and the enemy loses time trying to decide what action to take. In those vital seconds, the attack plane is finished and gone, having dropped its deadly warload.

If an aircraft is picked up successfully on radar screens when it is still about 25 miles away, ground units will have several minutes to track it, identify it, and get the air defense weapons on target. Then they will have only a few seconds to attack the plane and destroy it as it comes within range of guns or missiles. In reality, very few planes would be picked up that far away. Hills, trees, and valleys all provide places where aircraft can shield themselves from detection. Identifying whether the aircraft is friend or foe is usually done by electronic interrogation.

With the camouflage totally in place and the radar blended in with the background colors, this air defense site would be very difficult to spot even from a low-flying aircraft.

◀ This AN/TPS-63 tactical surveillance radar gives information about friendly and enemy aircraft and provides an air traffic control service for friendly pilots.

Air-to-air defense differs from ground defense because planes cannot carry the large, powerful radar sets that ground troops use with vehicles and trucks.
▼

An aircraft is picked up on the radar screen and observed to be approaching within strike distance of tanks and armored columns, artillery positions, or troop concentrations. A signal is sent on a fixed frequency to a small antenna on the plane. The plane receives that signal on a certain frequency and responds by sending back another signal, on a different frequency. That frequency basically says "I am a friend — do not shoot." If no signal comes back, the plane belongs to the enemy.

Having established whether the incoming plane is friendly or not, the ground defenses can prepare their response. If it is an enemy plane, they can prepare guns or missiles for action. In these days of automatic, computer-controlled missile batteries, it is tempting to believe that guns are outdated and that **surface-to-air missiles (SAMs)** are the way to defend ground units. That is not so. During the **Vietnam War** in the 1960s and early 1970s, more than 9,000 SAMs were fired by communist forces against U.S. and South Vietnamese planes. Only 150 planes were destroyed by these missiles.

Rapid-fire gun defenses play a crucial role in protecting army units from air attack. In one way, the missiles themselves have increased the value of guns for anti-aircraft work. Long-range missiles are capable of hitting high-flying planes; radar and missile units on the ground can track the planes and attack at leisure. The advent of long-range missiles forced a change in tactics, and since the 1970s, strike planes have flown low and fast. They are once again well within the range of gun defenses.

Ground-based air defenses shoot down more attacking planes than fighters do, and guns take a higher toll than missiles every time. In one five-year period in Vietnam, the United States lost 919 planes. Ground defenses brought down 827 of them, 763 by air defense gunfire and the rest by SAMs.

Air defense systems are frequently set up to provide protective screens for helicopter and light army aircraft operations.

In Vietnam, most SAMs used by the communists were old and their operators were not as skilled as professional soldiers in western countries. During the 1973 war in the Middle East between Israel and the Arab states, highly trained soldiers used modern equipment. On the average, missiles fired from fixed platforms on the ground shot down one plane for every 50 or 60 launched, while the several hundred shoulder-launched missiles destroyed only two aircraft. Shoulder-launched missiles are used by a single person and fired from a tube held over the shoulder.

The U.S. Army studies these records to determine which weapons are needed to protect the battlefield from air attack. A large number of short-range SAMs, many of them shoulder-launched, have been produced as cheap anti-aircraft defenses. Early missiles of this type homed in on the hot exhaust of a jet. That feature had one drawback. The plane had to be fired at from behind, after it had gone through and dropped its weapons.

More recent missiles were guided by a small control stick. The soldier used the stick to send signals to the speeding missile, keeping it on track as it chased the plane. The latest missiles of this type receive signals from a small camera. The operator keeps the camera pointed at the target, and a continuous signal is sent to the missile informing it of its own location and the location of the target.

When fired, Sidewinder air-to-air defense missiles, installed on fighters like this F-14, lock onto the hot exhaust of the enemy aircraft's engine. ▶

A Sidewinder closes in on a target plane after being fired from an F-14.
▼

MISSILE MEN

During the 1950s the U.S. Air Force developed a family of small, **infra-red missiles** called Sidewinder. Special detectors sensitive to infra-red radiation from hot objects enabled the missile to chase after the hot exhaust of enemy planes. Sidewinder was designed to be carried by fighter planes attacking other planes in the sky. The success of Sidewinder alerted the army to the possibilities of designing such a weapon for use by infantry as an anti-aircraft weapon.

Earlier methods for launching small, portable missiles involved a long wire through which the missile was guided to the low-flying aircraft. It proved almost impossible to get a direct hit because of difficulty in achieving such an accurate aim. The only part of the weapon even moderately lethal to flying aircraft was the trailing wire!

Developed during the 1950s, the Sidewinder family of small infra-red missiles uses special detectors sensitive to infra-red radiation from an aircraft's exhaust.

Sidewinder was successfully adapted for the increasing demands of air-to-air combat and provided the army with ideas for designing a similar weapon for infantry use.

Turning back to infra-red devices like those used on Sidewinder, the army developed an idea through a series of tests carried out in the late 1950s. General Dynamics was awarded a contract for the Redeye missile in 1959, and production got under way in the early 1960s. Production ceased in 1970, after about 100,000 Redeye missiles had been built. The Marine Corps also uses this missile, as do the armed forces of 11 foreign countries.

When it reached the army in the 1960s, Redeye was the world's first infantry SAM. It is light, only 29 pounds in the launch tube, and can be operated by one person. The missile itself is 4 feet in length, 2.75 inches in diameter, and weighs 18 pounds. It has four stabilizing fins at the rear and two small control vanes at the front. A small infra-red sensor in the glass nose of the missile "sees" the target when the infantryman puts the launch tube over his shoulder and points it in the appropriate direction. The soldier uses a sight on the side of the tube to aim the missile, and a buzzer sounds when the missile is ready to fire.

When the operator squeezes the trigger, a small boost charge fires inside the tube and the missile pops out at great speed. When the missile reaches a distance about twenty feet away from the operator its main rocket motor fires and it speeds away to its target. A tiny guidance device inside the missile keeps the hot target centered dead ahead and keeps the missile on course by sending instructions to the small guide vanes at the front. Redeye has a range of about two miles and reaches a top speed of about 1,800 MPH.

Work began in the 1970s on a replacement for Redeye that would overcome its limitations. The new missile was called Stinger. By changing the frequency at which the infra-red sensor "sees" the hot engine of the attacking plane, the infantryman can fire it before the plane goes past. He no longer needs to point the missile at the end of the jet plane's tailpipe. Now the infra-red seeker can lock on to the hot exhaust gases that trail some distance behind the plane. As the missile gets nearer the plane, a special guidance device inside steers it around to the plane's engine.

Sidewinder provides a defense against sudden attack by enemy planes.

The world's first successful surface-to-air missile specifically developed for infantry use was Redeye. It provided a light, ▶ *portable means of air defense for troops and small ground units.*

Portable air defense missiles like Stinger provide excellent protection for small ground units as they move quickly across areas less accessible to wheeled vehicles.

The missile is carried in a special launch pack fired from the shoulder. It weighs only 35 pounds. The missile itself is 5 feet long, with a diameter of 2.75 inches and a weight of 24 pounds. The explosive charge carried in the missile, much more powerful than that provided for Redeye, consists of a 6.6-pound charge with a proximity fuse. This fuse causes it to explode at a pre-set distance away from the target and makes sure some damage is done, even if the missile does not physically strike the plane. It might not strike it if the pilot takes evasive action.

Stinger has a range of just over three miles and an automatic interrogation device so the operator does not have to find out if the oncoming plane is friendly or not before he fires. This is a big advantage and means the

soldier does not have to determine the aircraft's nationality first. The missile refuses to fire if it picks up a friendly beacon signal. That little device could save a lot of American lives. In previous wars many planes have been shot down by friendly forces because gunners got excited and forgot to wait until they knew for certain that they were attacking an enemy aircraft.

Stinger's development period was long, and not until the early 1980s did the army receive its production model. The air force plans to buy a small number of Stingers for airfield defense against low-flying planes and helicopters. Several other countries have ordered Stinger, and the army says it wants about 50,000. About 15,000 had been delivered by the late 1980s.

Infantry moving across open country in armored personnel carriers receive extra protection from air defense units that are constantly on the lookout for enemy air threats.

VULCAN

Although we live in an age of missiles and push-button warfare, there is still a place for automatic anti-aircraft weapons with a high rate of fire, such as this Canadian 40mm Boffin air defense gun.

The standard U.S. Army air defense gun is the 20mm Vulcan rapid-fire cannon developed by General Electric. This gun is also used by the U.S. Air Force as an **air-to-air weapon** for attacking other planes. It has been in service with the army since 1968 and is used with the Chaparral SAM and usually carried on a tracked vehicle. Each air defense battalion has 24 Chaparral units working with 24 Vulcan self-propelled systems. The self-propelled model is mounted on the body of a modified M113 **armored personnel carrier**. Airborne divisions have a total of 48 towed Vulcan carriages pulled by trucks or tracked vehicles.

Vulcan is a good compromise between the limited capabilities of a hand-held missile and the mobile but less portable longer range missiles and guns.

The Vulcan air defense weapon operates on the gatling gun principle where several rotating barrels are clustered together, each firing as it aligns with the breech. ▼

The Vulcan fires fifty shells per second, and computers relay exact information from target tracking radar on how the gun should be pointed and fired.

The Vulcan is usually operated in conjunction with a special detection system called the forward area alerting radar, or TPQ-32, set up not far from the gun. This radar system provides information to the guns about where the targets have been seen. The radar antenna is mounted on the top of a mast capable of being raised to a height of about 36 feet. The dish is quite small, about 4 feet by 2 feet, 3 inches. It can detect aircraft as far away as twelve miles. This system can interrogate aircraft to decide whether they are friendly or not.

One drawback with guns is that once the rounds are fired they cannot change course to pursue a retreating aircraft. Only missiles have the advantage of changing course in mid-flight. To point the gun in precisely the right direction, the Vulcan is fitted with a fire control gunsight that observes and tracks the target. A small radar dish on the vehicle picks up the target that will first have been identified and categorized as a foe by the TPQ-32. This radar measures the range to the target, its speed, direction of travel, and how it is moving with respect to the gun.

This information is sent to the gun turret, where a computer analyzes how the gun should be pointed to hit the plane. This information is then used to align the gun and fire it. The Vulcan radar can pick up targets three miles away, and the capabilities of the fire control system can be improved with the addition of night sights or telescopic lenses.

The Vulcan gun itself is actually 6 barrels with a fire rate of up to 3,000 rounds per minute, which works out to 50 shells each round. The gun barrels are arranged in a cluster that rotates, each barrel firing in turn. This means that each barrel fires more than 8 rounds per second. Only small bursts are necessary to do lethal damage to a target. Gunners can select bursts of 10, 30, 60 or 100 rounds. Even the longest burst lasts only 2 seconds.

When used as an anti-aircraft weapon, the Vulcan gun has a maximum range of almost a mile. Because the barrels points upward, the rounds lose their momentum to gravity. The gun can, however, be used horizontally as an **anti-armor weapon** against light tanks and personnel carriers or vehicles. In this application it has a range of 2.8 miles. The army has about 380 self-propelled Vulcans and 220 towed versions.

Another means by which air defense can accompany fast-moving ground units is to mount radar, computing electronics, and missiles on a tracked vehicle, sometimes a converted tank chassis such as this Roland.

MOBILE MISSILES

Vulcan gatling guns are operated mainly in conjunction with the Chaparral surface-to-air weapon system. Developed from the early air force Sidewinder air-to-air combat missiles, Chaparral is 9 feet, 6 inches in length with a diameter of 5 inches and a weight of 185 pounds. It has four fins at the rear and guide vanes at the front for flight control. Maximum width across the rear fins is 25 inches. The missile has a single, solid-propellant rocket motor built by Rockwell.

Vulcan air defense gatling guns are sometimes operated along with Chaparral surface-to-air weapon systems developed from the Sidewinder.

▲
Some anti-aircraft missile systems have been designed for dual roles, like this system that can also be operated as an anti-tank weapon.

◄*Although it has some advantages, anti-aircraft/anti-tank systems complicate the very separate needs of air defense and anti-tank operations.*

Chaparral is carried on a turret and fired from rails to which it is held until ignition of the rocket motor. Unlike the shoulder-held Redeye and Stinger, Chaparral is not fired from a tube. Each turret mounting carries four Chaparrals and eight more rounds in the base for reloading after the first have been fired. The gunner sits on the turret and aims the missiles through an optical sight. Once fired, they will seek out the heat source of the aircraft and pursue it.

Chaparral comes in two principal mountings. It can be mounted on a lightweight truck towed by a military vehicle, or for additional mobility mounted on the top of an M730 tracked vehicle. The missiles can be fired manually using the optical sight, or they can work in conjunction with the **forward alert radars** set up with the Vulcan. Together, both gun and missile serve as an integrated air defense system.

40

Chaparral is by now quite old, although continuous modifications and improvements keep it reasonably effective. Yet it is no longer the right equipment for the job, and technical developments have left it behind as an inefficient system. Chaparral has a range of only three miles to a maximum altitude of 8,200 feet. The missile's warhead is a 28-pound high explosive. A much more effective army air defense weapon is the Improved Hawk, otherwise known as the MIM-23B. The original Hawk missile was developed in the 1950s as the first radar-guided air defense system. It was built to knock out low-flying aircraft and to provide protection for field units. It was cumbersome and very costly when first introduced, but the new version has improved performance and better radar.

The missile itself is 16 feet, 6 inches in length with a diameter of 14 inches. Hawk has four fins at the rear that double as stabilizers and flight control surfaces, working like the control surface of a plane to guide it through the air. Each missile weighs 1,383 pounds and contains a solid rocket motor made to fire in two phases. The first period of acceleration gets the missile up to high speed and generally on target. The next phase reduces acceleration and propels it to its target.

The Hawk air defense system is deployed widely as a surface-to-air protection for airfields and major ground bases.
▼

Patriot is a very flexible system and can attack aircraft up to 42 miles away. ▶

Hawk is capable of a 180 MPH interception speed and carries a 165-pound high-explosive warhead. It has a range of 25 miles and advanced radar guidance systems to lock onto a target identified by detection radars on the ground. The Hawk is frequently updated, and although it is quite old as a weapon system, it is the most widely used air-defense missile in the world. More than 40,000 have been built, and the missile has been exported to several countries.

The planned successor to Hawk and Improved Hawk is an impressive new missile called Patriot, which the army designates MIM-104. Patriot is classed as an advanced mobile battlefield SAM system. It is being built both to succeed the Hawks and to replace the Nike Hercules, a powerful but old anti-aircraft missile that first appeared in 1958. Nike Hercules could carry a nuclear warhead if required. It has a range of 93 miles and a top speed of more than 2,100 MPH.

◀ *The Patriot surface-to-air missile is fired in the general direction of the enemy aircraft and is then guided to its target by a computer.*

Patriot is an advanced mobile battlefield air defense system designed to replace the Improved Hawk and the few remaining Nike Hercules missiles first deployed in the late 1950s.
▼

The missile was built to combat high-flying supersonic aircraft, but it could operate only from fixed launch sites. When low flying became preferable over high flying, the missile was outclassed. Most U.S. Army Nike Hercules batteries were disbanded in the 1970s, but the missile is still operated, without the option of nuclear warheads, by several European countries and Japan.

In tune with the requirements of the modern army, Patriot is a much more flexible system. It is just over 17 feet in length and 16 inches in diameter. The missile weighs slightly more than 1 ton at launch and comes in canisters of four that can be towed or mounted on self-propelled vehicles. The missile is launched from its canister upon target information obtained by a special radar unit. This one radar unit combines all the separate functions provided by nine radar units operating the Hawk system. Patriot can knock out aircraft up to 42 miles away.

The British have developed this Rapier surface-to-air missile seen displayed in a courtyard at the Pentagon during 1985.

The army deploys this missile in the United States and Europe. Each battalion consists of six batteries equipped with eight canisters of four missiles. This provides a total of 192 missile tubes for each battalion. Production began in 1980 and about 2,100 missiles were delivered by the end of the decade. Patriot is part of a continuing test program and in one test was used to destroy a surface-to-surface battlefield missile. This demonstrates that the missile may have a role in knocking out missiles aimed at armored units on the ground.

Several other defense weapons have been developed and phased out because of cost and poor performance. One of these, the Roland, became so expensive it had to be canceled. Another, the Sergeant York, tried to copy an idea from the Soviets. U.S. observers had envied for many years the very effective Soviet ZSU-23 self-propelled air defense gun. It was a combination of the standard 23mm gun, simple radar units, and the chassis of an existing

vehicle. It was an effective combination and it works well today for Soviet air defense forces.

However, Sergeant York was canceled in 1985 because of technical problems and rising costs. The army is now analyzing which equipment it will need for short-range defense in the future. The ability of the ground forces to support battlefield operations rests on the quality of the air defense units. Without them, air power could seriously damage the efficiency of an entire army.

The Rapier is operated by a controller responsible for air defense radars from a protected vehicle or a concrete bunker.

GLOSSARY

Airborne reconnaissance	A survey from the air of enemy forces, equipment, and operations on and beyond the battlefield.
Air-to-air weapon	A gun or rocket used by aircraft for attacking enemy aircraft in the air.
Anti-armor weapon	A weapon designed to attack heavily armored vehicles, such as tanks and armored personnel carriers.
Armored personnel carriers	Tracked or wheeled vehicles protected with armor plate and used to carry soldiers or infantry men.
Forward alert radars	Radars set up on the ground to warn of incoming enemy air or land forces.
Gatling gun	A type of gun in which several barrels are positioned together in a cluster. As a barrel fires, the cluster rotates into position for the next barrel. This action continues while the gun is being used.
Infra-red missiles	Missiles that carry heat-seeking sensors for homing in on the hot engine exhaust of enemy aircraft.
Korean War	A war between 1950 and 1953 in which the United States repelled North Korean communist forces from invading South Korea.
Napalm	A jellied gasoline explosive contained in a bomb; when dropped, it spreads a flaming mass of gasoline over wide areas.
Radar	**Ra**dio **d**etection **a**nd **r**anging. A system of detecting objects by bouncing radio signals off them.
Remotely Piloted Vehicle (RPV)	A pilotless aircraft about the size of a model plane that carries cameras or electronic sensors for spying or intelligence-gathering.
Strike plane	An aircraft designed to attack ground targets in support of land operations.
Surface-to-Air Missiles (SAMs)	Missiles launched from the ground to attack aircraft in the air between short and long range.
Vietnam War	A conflict in Vietnam in which the U.S. armed forces assisted the national forces of the government of South Vietnam until it was overrun by communist North Vietnam in the early 1970s.

INDEX

Page references in *italics* indicate photographs or illustrations.